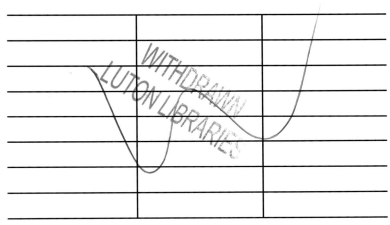

9 22000000 94 519

D1338380

Thomas Edison

PHYSICIST AND INVENTOR

Mary Boone

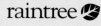

raintree
a Capstone company — publishers for children

Raintree is an imprint of Capstone Global Library Limited, a company incorporated in England and Wales having its registered office at 264 Banbury Road, Oxford, OX2 7DY – Registered company number: 6695582

www.raintree.co.uk
myorders@raintree.co.uk

Edited by Anna Butzer
Designed by Bobbie Nuytten
Picture research by Jo Miller
Production by Laura Manthe
Originated by Capstone Global Library Limited
Printed and bound in India.

ISBN 978 1 4747 5537 5
22 21 20 19 18
10 9 8 7 6 5 4 3 2 1

British Library Cataloguing in Publication Data
A full catalogue record for this book is available from the British Library.

Acknowledgements
We would like to thank the following for permission to reproduce photographs: Getty Images: Corbis Historical/Library of Congress, 21, The LIFE Picture Collection/David E. Scherman, 11; Library of Congress, 7; Newscom: Documenta/Album, 9, Mondadori Portfolio, 13, The Print Collector Heritage Images, 15, World History Archive, 17; Shutterstock: Everett Historical, cover (portrait), 5, 17 (inset), Marzolino, cover (lightbulb); The Image Works: Topham, 19

Design Elements: Shutterstock: SeDmi

Contents

CHAPTER 1

Young Edison

Have you ever turned on a light or watched a video? If so, your life has been touched by the **genius** of Thomas Alva Edison. He invented things we still use today. His inventions have changed over time. Thomas Edison's ideas are still seen almost everywhere.

genius remarkable talent or intelligence

Thomas in his laboratory, 1901

Thomas was born on 11 February 1847, in Milan, Ohio, USA. When he was 12, he started selling newspapers and snacks on a train. As a teenager he saved a toddler from a runaway train. The child's father thanked Thomas by teaching him to use a **telegraph**. This sparked Thomas' interest in **communications**.

Homeschooled

Thomas did not do well at school. He asked a lot of questions. This annoyed his teacher. The teacher said Thomas' brains were "addled", or scrambled. This angered Thomas' mother. She decided to teach him at home. Years later Thomas said that his mother "was the most enthusiastic champion a boy ever had".

telegraph machine that uses electronic signals to send messages over long distances

communications ways of sending information to people

Thomas, aged 14

CHAPTER 2

Curiosity leads to invention

Thomas started working as a telegraph operator when he was 15. In his spare time, he enjoyed taking things apart to see how they worked. His curiosity led him to **patent** his first invention when he was 20 – a vote counting machine. The machine worked, but it never caught on.

patent legal document giving an inventor sole rights to make and sell an item he or she invented

In 1869 Thomas moved to New York. He started an **engineering** company. In 1871 he invented a machine that printed **stock** prices. The Gold and Stock Telegraph Company bought the machine for $40,000. It was a lot of money at the time. Thomas had sold his first invention.

engineering using science to design and build things

stock share of a company that can be bought, sold or traded

The stock ticket printing machine Thomas invented

CHAPTER 3

The most famous inventions

Thomas invented thousands of things during his life. He may be best known for the light bulb. However, he did not invent the first light bulb. But he did develop the first light bulb that could safely be used in a home. He also invented switches that easily turned lights on and off.

FACT Before the light bulb, people burned candles or lamp oil. Electric lights were safer and easier to use.

Thomas holding a light bulb in his laboratory in Menlo Park, New Jersey, USA, 1910

13

Thomas knew a lot about the telegraph. This knowledge helped him invent the phonograph. The phonograph recorded and played back sound. It used needles and tin-covered **cylinders**. Thomas spent 52 years on this invention. The phonograph was patented in 1878.

"I always invented to obtain money to go on inventing."

Thomas Edison

cylinder shape with flat, circular ends and sides shaped like a tube

Thomas with his phonograph, 1878

Thomas and his employee WKL Dickson invented a film camera called the Strip Kinetograph. They also invented a way to watch the films by looking through a **peephole** viewer. They called it the Kinetoscope. In 1893 Thomas built a film studio. The studio made nearly 1,200 short films.

Hearing impairment

A childhood illness caused Thomas to lose most of his hearing. People asked him why he didn't invent a hearing aid. He often said he was working on one. But Thomas thought that being deaf helped him. He wasn't distracted from his work.

peephole small opening through which you can look

A man looks into a Kinetoscope, invented in 1889

CHAPTER 4

More inventions

Thomas was an excellent **physicist** and is known as one of the greatest inventors in the world. However, not all of Thomas' inventions were successful. Sometimes his ideas just didn't sell. One of these inventions was an electric pen. At other times it took a long time to get an invention right. He said it took him 1,000 tries to make a light bulb that worked.

"I have not failed. I've just found 10,000 ways that won't work."

Thomas Edison

physicist scientist who studies physics

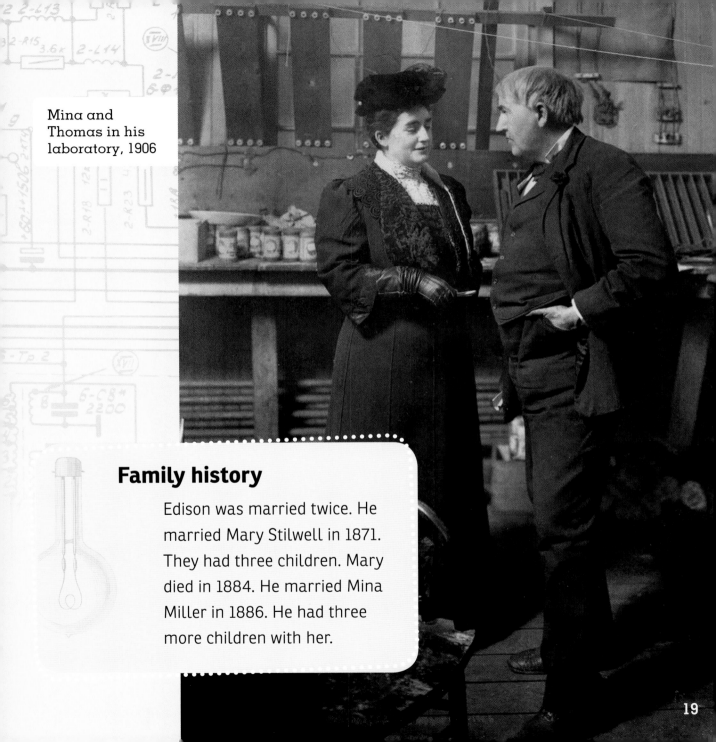

Mina and Thomas in his laboratory, 1906

Family history

Edison was married twice. He married Mary Stilwell in 1871. They had three children. Mary died in 1884. He married Mina Miller in 1886. He had three more children with her.

Even late in life, Thomas kept inventing. In 1912 car-maker Henry Ford asked Thomas to design a battery for the **Model T**. Thomas also invented an electric lamp for miners and a machine to view X-rays. Thomas died on 18 October 1931, in West Orange, New Jersey, USA. He was 94 years old.

FACT The Thomas Edison National Historical Park is in West Orange, New Jersey. Visitors can tour Edison's laboratories, libraries and home.

Model T early type of car made by the Ford Motor Company in 1908

Henry Ford (left) and
Thomas Edison, 1915

Glossary

communications ways of sending information to people

cylinder shape with flat, circular ends and sides shaped
  like a tube

engineering using science to design and build things

genius remarkable talent or intelligence

Model T early type of car made by the Ford Motor
  Company in 1908

patent legal document giving an inventor sole rights
  to make and sell an item he or she invented

peephole small opening through which you can look

physicist scientist who studies physics

stock share of a company that can be bought, sold
  or traded

telegraph machine that uses electronic signals to
  send messages over long distances

Find out more

Books

Inventions (100 Facts), Duncan Brewer (Miles Kelly, 2013)

Inventions (Tony Robinson's Weird World of Wonders), Tony Robinson (Macmillan Children's Books, 2013)

Thomas Edison (Science Biographies), Kay Barnham (Raintree, 2014)

Websites

www.bbc.co.uk/newsround/21995663
Find out about British inventor Joseph Swan's role in the story of the light bulb.

www.dkfindout.com/uk/science/famous-scientists/thomas-edison
Learn more about Thomas Edison. You can also take a quiz about Thomas and other famous scientists.

Comprehension questions

1. How do you think light bulbs have changed since Thomas Edison's day?

2. Thomas was good at marketing his inventions. Pretend you are Thomas in the 1890s. How would you advertise your new film camera and viewer?

3. Would Thomas have been as successful as he was if he lived today? Why or why not?

Index